EXPERIMENT WITH LIGHT

Written by Bryan Murphy

Science Consultant: Dr. Christine Sutton
Nuclear Physics Department, University of Oxford

Education Consultant: Ruth Bessant

Lerner Publications Company
Minneapolis, Minnesota

All words marked in **bold** can be found in the glossary that begins on page 30.

This edition published in 1991 by:
Lerner Publications Company
241 First Avenue North
Minneapolis, Minnesota 55401

Text © Bryan Murphy, 1991
Compilation copyright © Two-Can Publishing Ltd, 1991

First published in 1991 by:
Two-Can Publishing Ltd.
27 Cowper Street
London EC2A 4AP

Library of Congress Cataloging-in-Publication Data

Murphy, Bryan.
    Experiment with light / written by Bryan Murphy.
        p.   cm.
    "First published in 1991 by: Two-Can Publishing Ltd. . . . . London" — T.p. verso.
    Summary: Presents simple experiments demonstrating the basic scientific principles of light.
    ISBN 0-8225-2454-6
    1. Light — Juvenile literature. 2. Light — Experiments — Juvenile literature. [1. Light — Experiments. 2. Experiments.] I. Title.
QC360.M87   1991   91-8359
535'.078 — dc20   CIP
                                                       AC

Printed in Italy by Amadeus S.p.A. - Rome
Bound in the United States of America

1 2 3 4 5 6 7 8 9 10 00 99 98 97 96 95 94 93 92 91

ISBN: 0-8225-2454-6

All photographs are copyright © Fiona Pragoff, except for the following: front cover, pp. 4 (top), 11 (top), 12 (top), 22 (bottom right), 23 (top), 28 (top right), ZEFA Picture Library (UK) Ltd.; pp. 4 (bottom left), 7 (center right), J. Allan Cash Photolibrary; pp. 4 (bottom right), 10 (top), 26 (top right), Science Photo Library; pp. 5 (bottom right), 10 (bottom), 22 (top), NHPA; p. 10 (center left), Art Directors Photo Library; p. 15, Two-Can Publishing Ltd; and p. 22 (bottom left), Telegraph Colour Library.

All illustrations by Sally Kindberg.

CONTENTS

WHAT IS LIGHT?

What do you know about light? You cannot taste it, feel it, hear it, or smell it—but you can see it. Here are some interesting facts about light.

Light moves very fast. In one second, a beam of light can travel a distance equal to seven times around the Earth.

► Light is a form of **energy**. This house uses solar panels to convert the Sun's light into electric power.

▲ When something gets hot, it gives out light. Glowing coals in a fire give out red light.

▲ Stars may give out light that is red, yellow, white, or even blue. The color of a star depends on how hot it is.

▼ **Transparent** things, like clear water, allow light to pass straight through them.

▶ **Translucent** things, like frosted glass, scatter light and make things look blurry.

Light cannot go through **opaque** things, so you cannot see through them.

▶ Green plants make food from the energy contained in sunlight. When we eat plants, we take in some of this energy.

SUNDIALS AND ECLIPSES

Have you ever looked closely at your **shadow**? Where does it come from? When your body blocks the sunlight, a dark shadow falls on the ground. Is the shadow the same shape as your body, or does it look different? Why do you think this is?

◀ Try an experiment with your shadow. Stand so that your shadow falls on a sidewalk, and ask a friend to draw around it with chalk. Try the same thing against an upright wall. How is your shadow different?

Shadows do not always fall in the same place. As the Sun moves across the sky, shadows move as well. You can make a shadow clock, or **sundial**, to tell the time. All you need is a pencil, some modeling clay, and some cardboard.

Push one end of the pencil into the modeling clay and mount it near the edge of the cardboard so that it stands upright. This is your sundial.

Place the sundial on a sunny windowsill. The Sun will cast a shadow of the pencil onto the cardboard. Every hour, draw a mark where the shadow falls. At the end of the day, you will have a clock that never needs winding!

Remember to never look directly at the Sun. It can hurt your eyes.

If the Moon moves between the Sun and the Earth, it casts a giant shadow. This is called a **solar eclipse**. During a solar eclipse, all you can see of the Sun is its outline shining from behind the dark Moon.

Indoors, you can use shadows to make a picture called a **silhouette**. Have a friend stand sideways against a wall, and cast a shadow of your friend with a lamp. Carefully tape a piece of paper to the wall and trace the outline of the shadow. When you finish, you can cut out the shape, or you can color it in. Even though there is no detail, it should be easy to tell whose face it is.

A NAILHOLE CAMERA

Here is another way to draw with light. To make your own nailhole **camera,** you need only a few materials—an empty cardboard box, black paint, tracing paper, tape, a black cloth, and a nail. Ask an adult to help you make it.

Cut a rectangular hole from one side of the box, leaving a border about 1 inch (2½ centimeters) wide. Paint the inside of the box with black paint. Now use the nail to make a small hole opposite the large hole. When the paint has dried, tightly seal the top of the box and tape a sheet of tracing paper over the big hole.

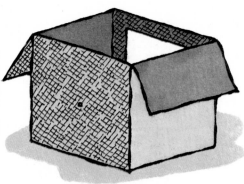

▲ Rest the camera on a steady surface. Now point the nailhole at a bright scene. The image, or picture, you see will be upside down but you can trace it.

To see the picture better, drape a dark cloth over your head and the side of the box with the big hole in it. Move the box to get a clearer image.

Carefully remove the tracing paper from the box and turn it over so that your picture is right side up. Now color it in.

Try making nailhole cameras with boxes of different sizes. Try using smaller or larger holes. If you make the nailhole bigger, the picture will be brighter, but it might be a little fuzzy.

BENDING LIGHT

Nearly all the light on the Earth comes from the Sun. Even moonlight is sunlight that has bounced off the Moon. Can you think of any other sources of light?

▲ Try looking at the stars on a very clear night. They look as if they are twinkling. This is because moving air bends the light, and the bending makes the light appear to move.

◀ On very hot days, there is a layer of hot air near the ground. This air can bend the sunlight that hits it, and you may see an image, called a **mirage**, floating in midair. Can you see a mirage behind the horses?

◀ The next time you go swimming, look at the bottom of the pool from above the water. The bottom may look closer to you than it really is. This is because the rays of light from above bend when they meet the water. When light bends, we say that it **refracts**.

▼ Here is another trick that you can do with bending light. Place a coin on the bottom of a shallow, opaque cup and have a friend stand just far enough away so that the coin is out of sight. Slowly fill the cup with water, and the coin will magically appear.

LIGHT AND LENSES

Many scientists use instruments such as **microscopes** to investigate tiny objects. Microscopes and **magnifying glasses** have **lenses** that are thicker in the middle than at the edges. Try looking at a blade of grass or an insect through a magnifying glass. What do you see?

What would you see through a lens that is thinner in the middle than at the edges? You can find out by looking through the eyeglasses of a **nearsighted** person. Can you see the difference? Do not wear someone else's eyeglasses for more than a few moments.

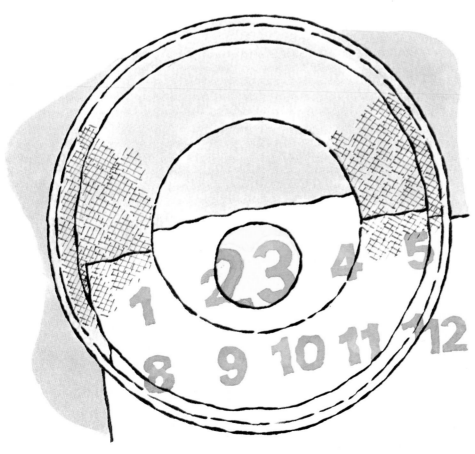

◀ Here is an experiment to make your own magnifying glass. You will need a transparent dish or cup, water, and some vegetable oil. First pour some water into the dish or cup. Then carefully pour a little oil on the surface of the water to form a small pool about ½ inch (1¼ cm) across.

Now put the dish over some printed type. If you look through the oil, the type looks bigger. You can **focus** the image by making the water deeper or shallower.

SNAP HAPPY

Do you have a camera of your own? If not, ask an adult if you can look at one to see how it works. Compare it to a nailhole camera. What differences do you see?

◀ Cameras come in all shapes and sizes, but almost all of them have five parts.

The *film* is where the image is fixed. It is coated with chemicals that react to light.

A *lightproof box* is the camera's shell. It is usually black inside to block out stray light.

The *lens* is a piece of curved glass or plastic. Light is focused through the lens to make an image on the film.

The *aperture* is a hole that can be made larger or smaller to let in different amounts of light.

The *shutter* opens to let light through the aperture.

◀ Automatic cameras adjust the lens, aperture, and shutter by themselves.

▶ Photographers have more control over their pictures if they can make their own adjustments.

Here are some tips to help you take good pictures.

- Remember to take off the lens cap!

- Make sure there is plenty of light if you are not using a flashbulb.

- If your camera needs focusing, be patient and focus accurately.

- Stand very still and keep the camera steady.

- Make sure that your subject fills the frame.

- Make sure that you can see heads, feet, and hands in the viewfinder.

- Keep your fingers and other objects away from the lens, or you could ruin your shot.

- Make sure the film is loaded into the camera properly.

- Do not point the camera at the Sun. Stand so that the Sun is behind you.

15

FOCUS ON EYES

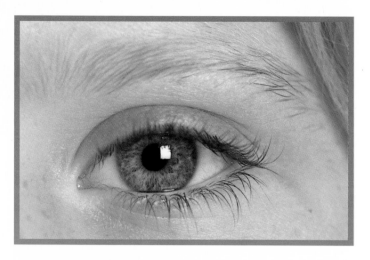

Your eyes are a little bit like cameras.

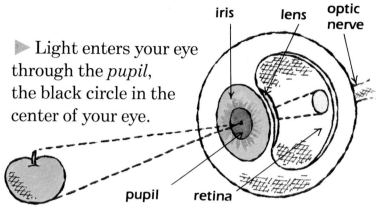

▶ Light enters your eye through the *pupil*, the black circle in the center of your eye.

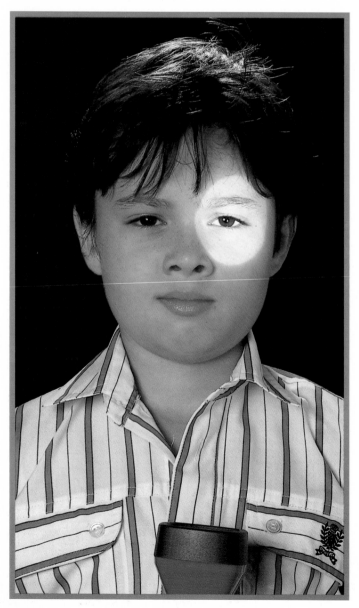

◀ Look at one of your friend's eyes. How big is the pupil? Now carefully shine a flashlight into your friend's eye and see what happens. Does the pupil change size? When it is dark, our pupils grow bigger to let in more light. When it is bright, our pupils get smaller because our eyes do not need as much light.

The *iris*, the colored part of your eye, changes the size of the pupil. This controls the amount of light that goes into your eye.

You have a *lens* in each eye that focuses light. Sometimes this lens does not work properly, and people need to wear an extra lens like eyeglasses or contact lenses.

Your eye's lens focuses light onto a surface called the *retina*. The images you see are upside down on your retina. Your *optic nerve* carries the image to your brain, which turns the picture right side up.

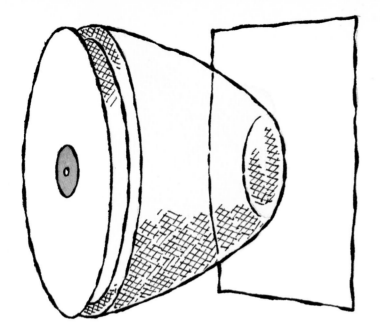

You can make a model of your eye using a round bowl made of clear glass, a sheet of white paper, and some cardboard. Cut a hole in the center of the cardboard about ½ inch (1¼ cm) across. This is the pupil. The glass bowl is like your eye. Point your model eye toward a television, with the cardboard facing the television screen.

Hold the sheet of paper behind the eye. This is like your retina. Move the model eye back and forth until you can see a good image of the television screen on the paper retina. Remember, the image will be upside down.

OPTICAL ILLUSIONS

You can fool your brain by looking at **optical illusions**. Optical illusions tell your brain to see an image one way, while your eyes see the image another way.

▶ Hold this page about 10 inches (25 cm) from your face and close your left eye. Look straight at the ant. You can still see the spider. Now, without taking your eye off the ant, slowly bring the page closer to your face. Suddenly the spider disappears! You have found your **blind spot**, where your eye joins your optic nerve. At your blind spot, your eyes cannot see light.

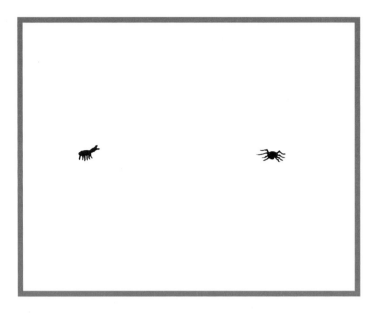

▼ What are these two friends looking at?

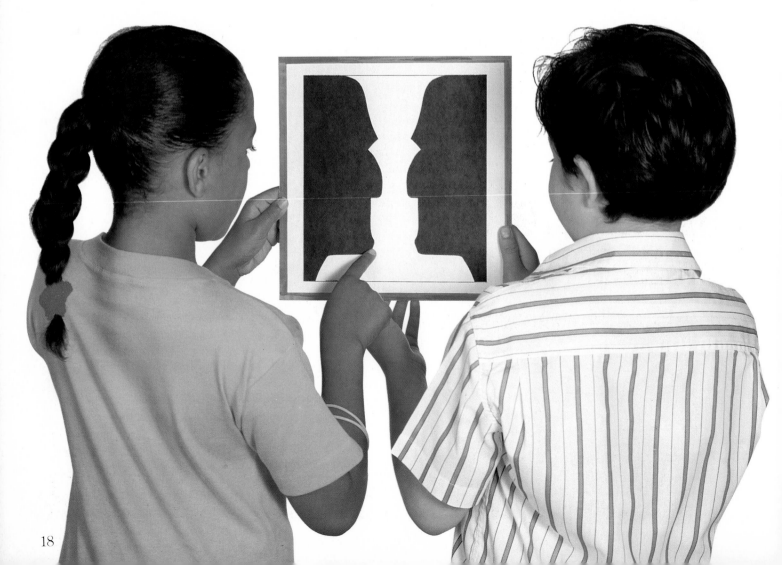

▼ Will the girl ever reach the top of this staircase?

▼ Which boy is the tallest?

▼ Can you see pale gray dots where the white lines meet?

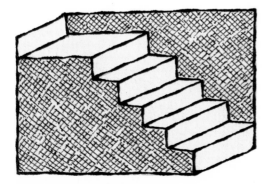

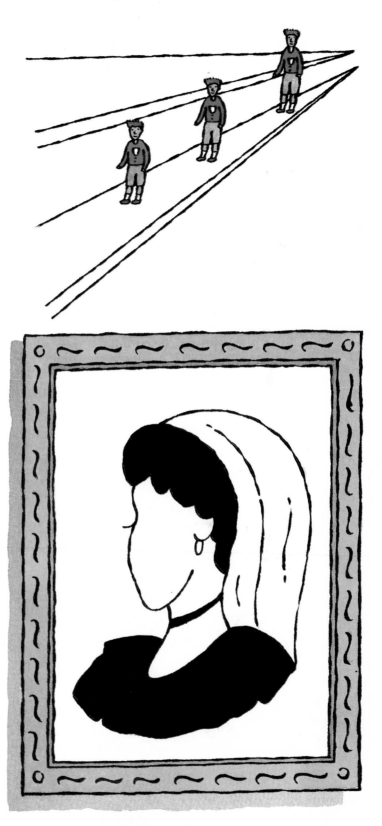

▼ Do you see the steps from above or below?

▲ Does the frame hold the portrait of a young woman wearing earrings or old woman with a large nose?

MIRROR MAGIC

Whenever light hits a very flat and smooth surface, it bounces off, or **reflects**. **Mirrors** reflect light. Try it and see!

Mirrors can be fun, and they can be useful. The mirrors on a car are placed in the center of the windshield and outside the front windows. These mirrors let drivers see all the vehicles on the road behind them.

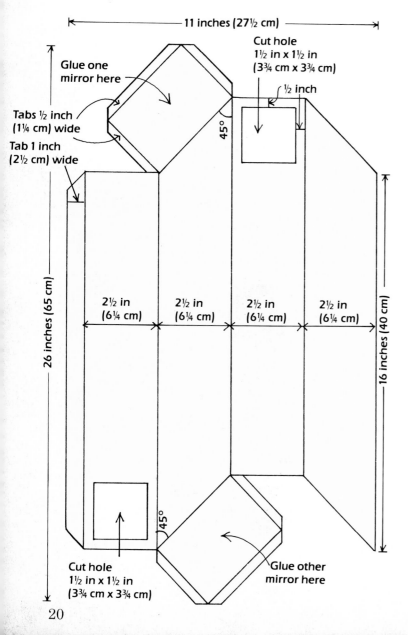

Do you sometimes wish that you could see over a wall without climbing it? You can with a **periscope**. You can even make your own periscope with two mirrors that measure about 2 x 3 inches (5 x 7½ cm), glue, and some cardboard. Ask an adult to help you make it.

◀ Draw this shape onto cardboard and cut it out. Glue the mirrors in position and apply glue to the tabs. Then fold the cardboard into a long, narrow box.

▶ Now you can look around corners and over walls without being seen.

Look for other mirrors at home. Some are flat, and some are curved. A spoon is like a mirror. Look at your reflection in each side of a spoon. Which side makes you look upside down?

THE COLORS
OF THE RAINBOW

Imagine a whole world without color. We would see gray skies, gray grass, and gray flowers. Many animals and plants would not survive, because different colors send important signals to them.

Colors make flowers stand out, so that insects will eat the nectar inside the flowers and spread pollen that makes new flowers grow.

▼ Many animals and birds, like this beautiful peacock, use bright colors to attract a mate.

▲ Other animals use colors to hide from their enemies. Chameleons can change the color of their skin to blend in with the plants or rocks around them.

Rainbow colors

red

orange

yellow

green

blue

indigo

violet

▲ Sunlight is made up of many colors. Usually, the colors combine and look white. But if the Sun is shining and it is raining at the same time, the raindrops split the light into different colors. Then you can see a huge band of color called a **rainbow**.

◀ You can make your own rainbow on a sunny day. Put your finger over the end of a garden hose to make a very fine spray. If you stand with the Sun behind you, you can see all the colors of the rainbow in the water.

Grass looks green because it reflects green light. It soaks in all the other colors. An apple looks red because it reflects red light. On a sunny day, black things get hot because they soak in all the Sun's light. White things stay cooler because white reflects all colors.

COLOR DISKS

What do you think would happen if you mixed together all the colors of the rainbow?

Cut out a circle from cardboard and draw lines through it to divide it into six equal sections. Color the sections red, orange, yellow, green, blue, and purple. Make two holes at the middle of the disk, ½ inch (1¼ cm) apart, and thread about 30 inches (75 cm) of string through them. Tie the ends together and loop the string over your middle fingers. Spin the disk to wind the string. Pull your hands apart, then move them closer together. The disk will spin very quickly, and the spinning disk will wind the string again.

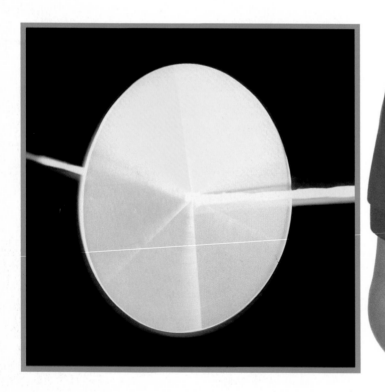

▲ What does the disk look like when it is spinning quickly? Instead of looking colorful, the disk will look almost white. This is because the separate colors move so quickly that your eyes get confused and mix them together.

On the other side of the disk, draw lines to make three equal sections. Color the sections red, green, and blue. Does this side also look grayish-white when it spins? Try making disks with only two colors on them. Color one red and green, one red and blue, and one blue and green. What color does each spinning disk look like?

WORLDS WITHOUT COLOR

Some people are **color-blind**, which means they cannot see colors very well. Most people who are color-blind cannot see the difference between the different shades of red and green. Can you see any numbers in this circle? People with red and green color blindness cannot see them.

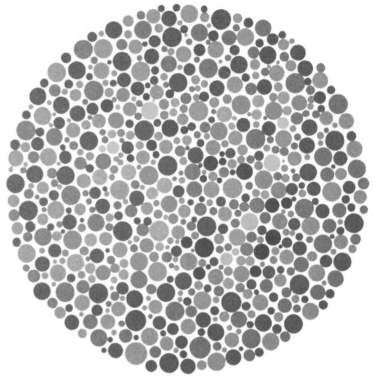

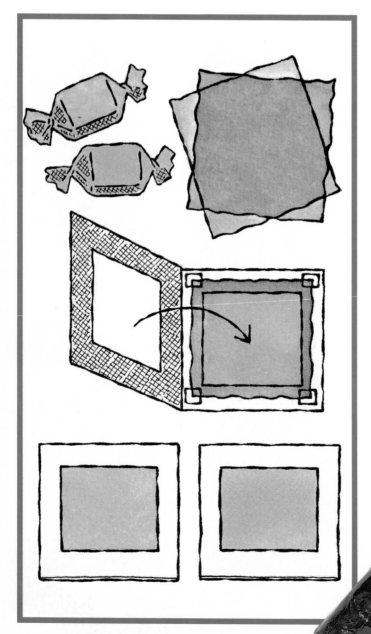

◀ You can change the colors of things you see by looking through a piece of thin colored plastic called a **filter**. You can make your own filters from colored candy wrappers. Mount them in cardboard frames. Try looking through a red one. Anything that is red, yellow, or orange should look light, while other colors will look dark. This is because filters only let certain colors of light pass through them. What does the sky look like through the filter? Photographers often use red or orange filters when they take pictures outdoors.

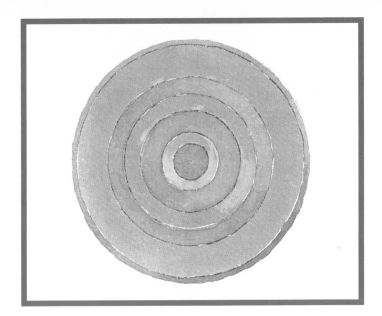

Put a green filter in front of your left eye and a red one in front of your right eye. Look at the pictures on this page with one eye closed. Now try it using the other eye. Do the filters change what you see?

COLOR TELEVISION

Have you ever thought about how a television picture is made? The next time you are watching your favorite program, look closely at the screen.

▼ The picture is made up of little dots of light. Can you see what colors they are? There are only red, green, and blue dots. How can all the different colors you see in a television picture be made up of just three colors?

Mixing paints

red + green = brown

green + blue = turquoise

red + blue = purple

red + green + blue = black

If you move away from the screen, you can see that the light from the different dots mixes together to produce a full-color picture.

▶ Mixing paints is not like mixing light. You may know that the **primary colors** of paint are red, blue, and yellow. Light has different primary colors. They are red, blue, and green.

27

A red part of the television picture is made up of only red dots. A blue part of the picture has only the blue dots glowing. A green part of the picture has only the green dots glowing.

A turquoise part of the picture is made with green and blue dots.

A purple part of the picture is made with red and blue dots.

A yellow part of the picture is made with red and green dots.

A white part is made up of all three dots of light—red, blue, and green.

29

GLOSSARY

blind spot: the part of your eye that cannot see light

camera: a machine that takes photographs by focusing light onto film

color-blind: unable to see the difference between certain colors, such as red and green

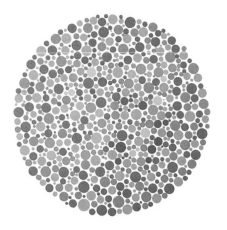

energy: the power to do work

filter: a piece of colored glass or plastic that lets only certain light rays through

focus: to adjust a lens in order to make an image clear

lens: a piece of curved glass or plastic that focuses light

magnifying glass: a lens that makes things look bigger

microscope: an instrument that uses two or more lenses to make very small things look much bigger

mirage: a false image seen when light is bent by hot air

mirror: a smooth surface, usually made of glass, that reflects light

nearsighted: able to see things that are near more clearly than things that are far away

opaque: letting no light through

optical illusion: an image that tells your brain one thing and tells your eye something else

periscope: a tube with two mirrors that lets you see around corners or over high walls. Periscopes are used in submarines to see above the surface of the water.

primary colors: a set of colors that can be mixed together to make all other colors. The primary colors of light are red, blue, and green.

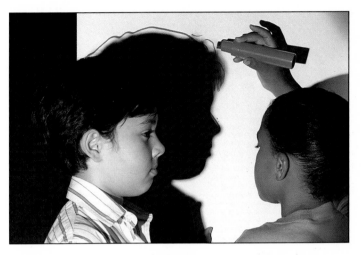

rainbow: a curved band of colors, seen when light goes through falling rain or mist

reflect: to bounce light off a surface

refract: to bend light on a surface

shadow: the dark area that is created when an object blocks rays of light

silhouette: an outline drawing

solar eclipse: the time when the Moon moves between the Sun and the Earth and blocks out the Sun's light

sundial: a clock that measures the position of shadows to tell the time of day

translucent: allowing some light to shine through, but scattering it so that images are blurred

transparent: letting light pass through

INDEX